A Lollygag of Limericks

ALSO BY MYRA COHN LIVINGSTON

Come Away
    (*A Margaret K. McElderry Book*)
4-Way Stop and Other Poems
Happy Birthday!
I'm Hiding
The Malibu and Other Poems
    (*A Margaret K. McElderry Book*)
The Moon and a Star and Other Poems
The Way Things Are and Other Poems
    (*A Margaret K. McElderry Book*)
When You Are Alone/It Keeps You Capone:
    An Approach to Creative Writing with Children
    (*A Margaret K. McElderry Book*)
Wide Awake and Other Poems
    (*A Margaret K. McElderry Book*)

EDITED BY MYRA COHN LIVINGSTON

Listen, Children, Listen: Poems for the Very Young
O Frabjous Day: Poetry for Holidays and
    Special Occasions
    (*A Margaret K. McElderry Book*)
One Little Room, An Everywhere: Poems of Love
The Poems of Lewis Carroll
Speak Roughly to Your Little Boy: A Collection of
    Parodies and Burlesques, Together with the Original
    Poems, Chosen and Annotated for Young People
A Tune Beyond Us: A Collection of Poems
What a Wonderful Bird the Frog Are: An Assortment of
    Humorous Poetry and Verse
    (*A Margaret K. McElderry Book*)

MYRA COHN LIVINGSTON

A Lollygag of Limericks

with drawings by JOSEPH LOW

A MARGARET K. MCELDERRY BOOK

ATHENEUM   1980   NEW YORK

Library of Congress Cataloging in Publication Data

Livingston, Myra Cohn.
A lollygag of limericks.
"A Margaret K. McElderry book."
SUMMARY: A collection of limericks based
on English place names.
1.   Limericks—Juvenile literature.   [1.   Limericks]
I.   Low, Joseph, 1911–   II.   Title.
PZ8.3.L75Lo   811'.5'4   77–18060
ISBN 0–689–50104–8

To Dick, Jan, Judy and Morley—
lollygaggers of Summer, 1976

Said an old man from Needles-on-Stoor,
"I eat all of my meals on the floor;
   Though I'm perfectly able
   To sit at the table,
I find it a terrible bore."

Cried a man on the Salisbury Plain,
"Don't disturb me—I'm counting the rain;
  Should you cause me to stop
  I might miss half-a-drop
And would have to start over again."

Wailed a ghost in a graveyard at Kew,
"Oh my friends are so fleeting and few,
   For it's gravely apparent
   That if you're transparent
There is no one who knows if it's *you*!"

A lazy old grocer of Eyer
Once noticed his shop was on fire.
  "But no matter," he said,
  "I'll just stay home in bed,
And when it burns down, I'll retire."

A frightened soothsayer from Ryde
Exclaimed, "It is hard to decide
   If my stars are propitious
   Or most inauspicious
And so I don't venture outside."

In a roostery somewhere near Fen
Clucked a selfish and lazy old hen,
 "If I stand on one leg
 I will lay half-an-egg
And they'll never disturb me again."

There was a young fellow of Stroud
Who dressed himself up in a shroud.
    When they called him a freak
    He replied, "I'm unique
And don't wish to be one of the crowd."

Said a gluttonous man of New Wales,
"Since I've eaten a bevy of quails,
   A small sownder of swine
   And a drove of young kine,
Would you *please* help me finish the snails?"

There was once a young fellow of Wall
Who grew up so gigantically tall
   That his friends dug a pit
   Where he'd comfortably sit
When he wished to converse with them all.

A certain old widow of Chipping
Declared that her memory was slipping;
   "I'm not certain," said she,
   "If there's cream in my tea
Or there's tea in the cream I've been sipping."

Said a serious scholar from Leech,
"I have written a glorious speech
    Which will clearly explain
    Who invented the rain
And taught all of the barn owls to screech.

"Furthermore, it will set matters right
As to why daytime differs from night,
    Who discovered the tree
    And conceived of the bee,
And, in essence, why *I* am so bright!"

A discerning young lamb of Long Sutton
Begged his grandfather, "Don't be a glutton;
    For you eat up the grass
    In a manner so crass
That they'll soon have you carved up as mutton."

Said a three-day-old infant in Leek,
"There are matters of which I must speak
   Erudite and profound,
   Which I plan to expound
When I've been on the earth for a week."

A man on the Isle of Wight
Complained his left shoe was too tight;
　　Whereupon he resolved
　　This was easily solved
By exchanging the left for the right.

Said a restless young person of Yew,
"I will purchase a nice kangaroo;
    I can sit in her pouch
    And pretend it's a couch
And wherever she hops, I will too!"

A confectioner living in Skittle
Once confessed, "I'm so skinny and little
    That unless I put glue
    On the sole of my shoe
I'd fall into my own peanut brittle."

Cried a maid in the Manor at Foss,
"This old building is making me cross!
   I am covered with dust,
   Several cobwebs and rust,
Not to mention great patches of moss."

A person of Stow-on-the-Wold
Complained it was growing so cold
   That he put on three suits,
   Seven hats and six boots
And smothered himself, I am told.

Said a poor girl from Southend-on-Sea,
"I've decided to sleep on a pea,
For if stories are true
I will turn black and blue
And they'll know the true princess is *me*!"

A meticulous person of Grange
Once declared, "Though my friends think me strange
   Teaching roosters to crow
   And the weeds how to grow,
They would be most confused should I change."

A venturesome woman of Kent
Scattered perfume wherever she went,
   For said she, "Should I stray
   And get lost on the way,
They can find me by tracing my scent."

Called a boatman at Charing Cross Pier,
"If you'll just hop aboard, I can steer
  Thrice and back to the Tower
  In less than an hour,
Though it's certain to make you feel queer."

A ribald old parrot of Cuffley
Explained, "If I speak rather toughly,
   If I swear and I curse,
   Put the blame on my nurse,
Who raised me uncommonly roughly."

A kind woman quite near Barnby Moor
Folded all of her rugs in a drawer;
   When they said, "Are you daft?"
   She replied, "There's a draught
And they've asked to get up off the floor."

A pompous old donkey of Yately
Walked about with his head held sedately;
　　When they said, "Tell us why?"
　　He would stiffly reply,
"It enhances my image so greatly."

There was a young woman of Brighton
Who slept every night with her light on:
    "It is not," she declared,
    "That I'm skittish or scared—
Just the slightest bit easy to frighten."

An artistic young person of Churt
Smudged some charcoal all over his shirt;
   When they cried, "Oh, how queer!"
   He replied with a sneer,
"Gracious yes, but it won't show the dirt!"

A forgetful young woman of Tring
Tied up all of her fingers with string.
    "But," said she, "my poor brain's
    Growing addled again
And I don't know which knot's for what thing!"

A small mouse in Middleton Stoney
Grew pitifully skinny and bony;
   "It's apparent," he said,
   "I'm improperly fed
On a diet of raw macaroni."

Said a guide walking round Lacock Abbey,
"Though you now find me cordial and gabby,
    You would back off in fright
    Should you see me at night
For at home I grow silent and crabby."

An affectionate fellow in Cheddar
Fell in love with a kitten and fed her;
   "O I'll bed her in silk
   And I'll keep her in milk,
But I'm perfectly sure I shan't wed her."

A fine lady of Gorley on Thames
With a passionate fondness for gems
    Was so frightened of thieves
    She hid pearls in her sleeves
And sewed bracelets and rings in her hems.